D1478026

A Guide to
Underwater Communication

Florida, Bahamas and Caribbean Edition

Keith A. Ellenbogen

Blue Reef Publications, Inc., Newton, Massachusetts

To my Father, who has been supportive every step of the way.

Published by: **BLUE REEF PUBLICATIONS, INC.**
Post Office Box 42
Newton Centre, MA. 02159 USA
617-332-7965   FAX 617-332-7967

Photographs Copyright© by EarthWater Stock photographers:
Curtis Boggs, Chris Crumley, David Cubbin, Hans Graspointner, Tim Grollimund, Stan Kidd, Douglas David Seifert, Michele C. Sistrunk, Martin Sutton

The author expresses thanks to ImageSet Design for its contributions.

Scuba Talk™ is a trademark of Blue Reef Publications, Inc.
Diver's Pearl™ is a trademark of Blue Reef Publications, Inc.

ISBN 0-9645407-4-6
Library of Congress Catalog Card Number: 95-94363

Made in the United States of America

TABLE OF CONTENTS

Introduction:

Underwater communication is a troublesome experience for most divers, particularly for the recreational diver who often has a real need to communicate but no underwater "language" to use—until now.

Designed specifically for the recreational diver, Scuba Talk will teach you a system of carefully devised hand signals which will enable you to identify and communicate a sighting of a particular fish or undersea animal to your dive partner. Divers who use these hand signals report that this new underwater vocabulary truly enriches their dive experience. Scuba Talk also includes a set of practical signals to communicate location, intention, and safety issues. Hence, for many divers, underwater vocabulary is not only enriching but essential to their dive experience.

This edition of Scuba Talk covers the waters of the Caribbean, Bahamas, Florida Keys, and the Gulf of Mexico, including Cancun and Cozumel. Inside you'll find a hand signal plus detailed information on the most spectacular fish and animals in this region. From sharks to goatfish, to crabs to eels to rays, Scuba Talk gives you both fascinating facts and diving advice, as well as a way to communicate these sightings to your diving partners.

Inside Scuba Talk you'll also find a diver's log book, pre-dive check list, address book (scuba buddies), personal identification card, and a log book to record all of your sightings.

Above all, Scuba Talk aims to enrich your dives. As a diver, you already know that being underwater is one of life's great experiences. Being able to share that experience with a diving partner makes a dive even more satisfying—which is what this book is all about. Dive often and enjoy!

What's in Scuba Talk:

A "scuber" (user) friendly book!

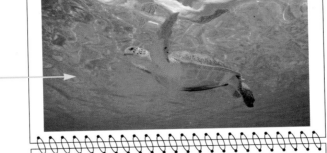

Easily Identifiable Photograph →

General Information →

Scuba Talk HAND SIGNAL

SEA TURTLE

← **Unique Hand Signal**

DIVER'S PEARL

Interesting Facts →

PART ONE

SHARK

Reef Sharks

The sighting of a shark

is the underwater thrill of a lifetime. Being in the presence of these skilled predators strikes both fear and admiration in divers for one of the most mysterious and awesome underwater animals.

Sharks can detect motion from over 100 feet by using a sensory organ called the lateral line system which detects vibrations in the water. The shark also possesses a remarkable sense of smell. Two-thirds of its brain is devoted to detecting smells. In fact, sharks can detect drops of blood from a quarter-mile away.

Sharks also have excellent hearing and are able to hear a struggling animal up to 1000 meters away. In addition to remarkable senses of sight, taste, touch, smell and hearing, sharks also possess a sixth sense of registering electrical signals which are helpful in navigation and obtaining prey.

Sharks differ from other fish in many ways. Instead of bones, their skeletons are made up of cartilage, a tough elastic substance. Also, sharks lack a swim bladder. Most species of sharks would sink to the bottom if they stopped swimming. However, to compensate for the absence of a swim bladder, sharks have an oversized, oil-rich liver, which increases their buoyancy. Shark's teeth are embedded in their gums and are not attached to their jaws. The shark possesses several rows of teeth which are constantly replacing each other.

Unfortunately, this beautiful animal has been portrayed by Hollywood and the media as a vicious man-eater. Out of the more than 250 species of sharks, only a handful are considered dangerous to man, and shark attacks are uncommon. It is a magnificent creature which should be admired not destroyed.

DIVER'S PEARLS

1. The largest fish in the world is the whale shark, which can measure approximately 60 feet in length and weigh up to 15 tons. It is a harmless shark that feeds peacefully on plankton.

2. Sharks can swim extremely fast. The blue shark was recorded at a burst speed of 43 MPH.

3. Shark skin, *shagreen*, was at one time used as sandpaper.

RAY

Manta Ray

"It's a bird! It's a plane!

No, it's a RAY!" Rays move their wings in a balletic undulating motion, appearing to fly through the ocean. All rays have pectoral fins which have adapted to form a wing-like shape. To prevent drawing in sandy water from life on the sea floor, rays have evolved a clever adaptation that ensures clean water. Spiracles, one-way valves on the top of the ray's body near the eyes, draw water in and pump it through the gills on the underside of the body. However, certain rays, such as the manta ray, are pelagic (live in the open sea). Pelagic rays breathe the way most fish breathe.

These adaptations allow rays to lie virtually unnoticed or cruise the sandy bottom to search for foods such as clams, oysters, shellfish and a variety of small fish.

Rays are close relatives to sharks. Both possess cartilaginous skeletons and gill slits instead of the gill covers that are found on most boney fish.

Southern Stingray

Stingrays

"Stingray city", located in the Cayman Islands, is the place to go if you want to see the large southern stingray (*Dasyatis americana*). Stingrays spend much of their time camouflaged in the sandy bottom. As the name suggests, stingrays do have a stinger located on their tails which can inject poison into human flesh. Fortunately, these rays almost never attack unless they are provoked by someone stepping on or abusing them.

Eagle rays

Eagle rays are named after their resemblance to eagles. Unlike most rays, their pectoral fins do not extend to their heads, thus leaving a profile of a head, snout, and large brown eyes similar in appearance to an eagle. Eagle rays also possess stingers on their tails. Although they seldom sting, they are potentially dangerous. They are seen swimming alone or in groups. Eagle rays' wing spans can reach a size of up to 15 feet.

Spotted Eagle Ray

Manta rays

The manta ray was nicknamed the "devil fish" by ancient pearl divers, who believed a manta ray would blanket a person under the darkness of its giant wing span (22 ft.) before devouring him.

Contrary to old beliefs, the manta ray is a peaceful, curious animal which appears to enjoy swimming in the presence of divers. The manta ray uses its two front fins as a scoop to feed constantly on the mass of small drifting animal and plant life called plankton.

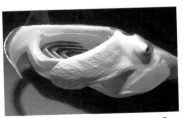
Manta Ray

Gold Spotted Moray

Scuba Talk HAND SIGNAL

EEL

EEL

The moray eel is another fish which has received an undeserved reputation as a dangerous animal. This fish is a shy, nocturnal animal. The eel breathes by opening and closing its mouth, thereby forcing water through its gills. Morays do possess sharp teeth, powerful jaws, and extremely fast reflexes. Morays are usually seen peacefully hanging out in a small coral hiding place, which it calls home. As with any homeowner, people who try to pet a moray, or stick a hand into its home, are putting themselves at risk. Many animals' livelihoods depend on their ability to attack in response to a threat. This is especially true in the coral reef ecosystem.

As a diver, it is a great thrill to stop and watch a moray relaxing in his home. These fish seem to hypnotize you with the opening and closing of their mouths. An even more spectacular sight is watching the moray swim in a snake-like manner in search of its favorite prey—octopus and lobsters. This is usually seen at night when morays are most active.

DIVER'S PEARLS

1. The true color of the green moray is brown. However, its brown skin is usually blanketed by a film of green algae, giving it a green appearance.

2. A moray's skin is thick and scaleless.

3. Don't Pet!

Green Moray

13

Balloonfish

BLOWFISH

Commonly referred to as pufferfish—there are actually several species which have this ability to "puff up"—examples of this group are: pufferfish, burrfish, porcupinefish, and ballonfish. Therefore, when spotting a fish of this kind, the proper general terminology is blowfish (unless you know the exact species you're looking at).

Blowfish have developed an extraordinary survival technique. When threatened (usually just before being eaten), they ingest water to enlarge their bodies up to three times original size. In addition to making themselves larger, their spines point outward, making them unappetizing to potential predators. But that is only part of their defense. Blowfish also produce poisonous neurotoxin. As a result, they can swim confidently through the water—no worries.

Balloonfish (puffed)

DIVER'S PEARLS

1. In Japan, the meat of a particular pufferfish (*Arothron tetradon*) is considered an aphrodisiac. However, if prepared incorrectly, the ingested neurotoxin can be fatal. Are you willing to try this?

2. Appreciate these fish for their exotic nature, but please do not agitate them in order to elicit a response. In point of fact, this puffing defense mechanism stresses their body substantially—shortening their life expectancy.

Scuba Talk HAND SIGNAL

BLOWFISH

ANGELFISH

"Poetry in motion" is the phrase that best depicts the movements of the **angelfish**. One of the most graceful species, the angelfish is worth a second look.

View the angelfish broadside—and get your camera ready—or you're likely to miss it. The angelfish has some of the most beautiful color patterns of any fish. Bright colors are usually associated with warnings to potential predators. However, in the case of the angelfish, its brilliant colors seem to be used to settle territorial disputes between members of its own species.

As a result, juvenile angelfish are usually less colorful then their parents. The adult angelfish are territorial and can not tolerate other members of their species in their home turf. The less colorful juveniles are not seen as a threat and therefore are permitted to live in the same area as their parents.

Juvenile Queen Angelfish

Scuba Talk HAND SIGNAL

ANGELFISH

Gray Angelfish

17

TRUMPETFISH

As seen in the photograph, trumpetfish have long thin bodies. This particular species (*Aulostomus maculatus*) can reach a size of up to two ft. Commonly seen hovering near corals for camouflage, the trumpetfish is a spectacular sight for divers.

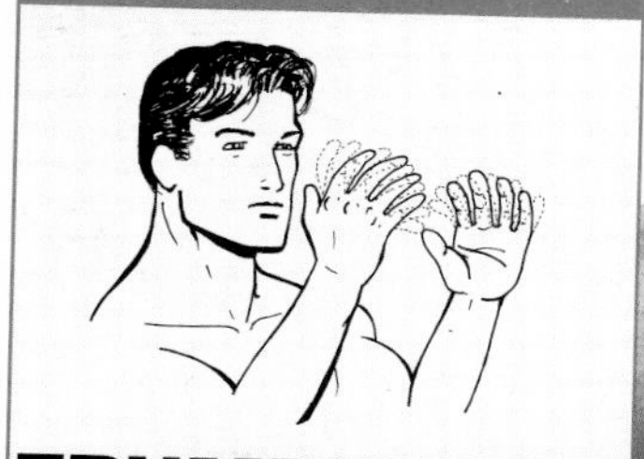

TRUMPETFISH

Scuba Talk HAND SIGNAL

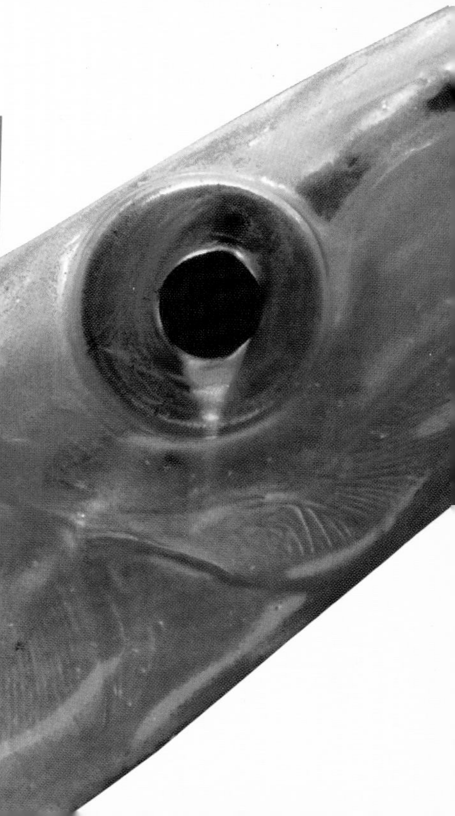

Stop and spend a moment watching the trumpetfish on the prowl. Trumpetfish have been known to camouflage half their bodies to resemble the surrounding environment, such as coral or grass, while their heads change to another color to match the small fish they hunt. This camouflaging tricks their prey into thinking they are among friends, not foes. As the trumpetfish completes the hunt by snapping up the small fish in its large trumpet-like mouth, it sets forth the evolutionary chain, as well as the famous quote "larger fish eat smaller fish".

DIVER'S PEARL

Test your hovering abilities by trying to match the trumpetfish as it remains motionless.

Hawksbill Turtle

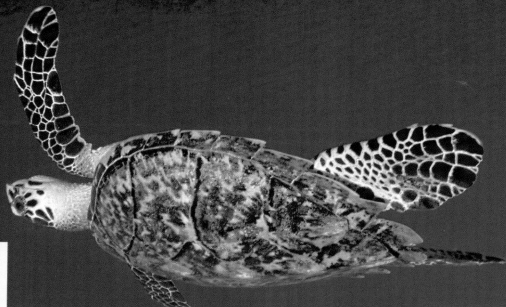

SEA TURTLE

Scuba Talk HAND SIGNAL

SEA TURTLE

Sea turtles are large, air-breathing reptiles. Over millions of years, sea turtles have adapted to ocean life, returning to land only to lay their eggs. Spotting a sea turtle is truly an occasion for celebration. These graceful animals glide through the water and sometimes surprise divers by swimming right next to them. Don't try to out swim a sea turtle, as they are fast. Just stop and watch the animal move effortlessly through the water, using its front feet as flippers.

Unfortunately, the sea turtle's beauty has lured many hunters. In the sixteenth century, and still to this day, sea turtles are hunted for shells, meat, cosmetic oils, and leather. Today, getting trapped in fishermen's nets is its greatest danger. All sea turtles are either endangered or threatened animals. Help is needed. Fortunately, legislation is pushing fishermen in the Gulf of Mexico to install a Turtle Extruder Device (TED) in all fishing nets to help prevent unnecessary deaths.

DIVER'S PEARL

Ever wonder why you never see a baby sea turtle? Well, so do scientists. The truth is that no one knows exactly what happens to a baby sea turtle until it reaches its adult size.

OCTOPUS

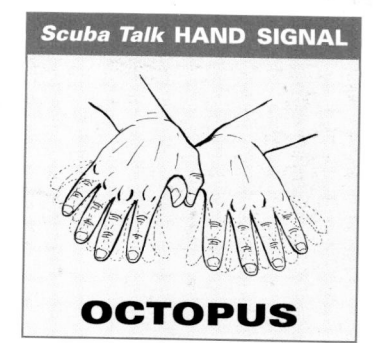

Scuba Talk HAND SIGNAL

OCTOPUS

The **octopus** is fairly common but rarely spotted. The octopus is not a fish; rather, it belongs to a group of shellfish called mollusks, which also includes clams, oysters, and snails.

The octopus, with its highly developed brain and nervous system, can outsmart even the best of us. This animal has the ability to change color patterns to show moods like aggression and fear. Octopus can also change the texture of their skin to match the surrounding environment of corals and rocks.

It is the octopus' tough mantle (outer skin) which gives the animal its shape. The octopus can maneuver its body through the smallest crack. In fact, the only bone in the octopus' body is its beak-like mouth. The octopus is certainly a rare sight for divers, and even when spotted they quickly disappear. However, if you look closely and are lucky, you may encounter this amazing animal.

DIVER'S PEARLS

1. The word "octopus" comes from two Greek words meaning "eight feet."

2. Octopus in your fish chowder? Send it back, it belongs in clam chowder. (Don't forget, it's a mollusk!)

Caribbean Reef Octopus

PARROTFISH

Scuba Talk HAND SIGNAL

PARROTFISH

*Stoplight Parrotfish
(initial phase)*

"What colors!" The **parrotfish** is one of the most colorful fish seen by divers, with its magnificent blue, green, red and black color configurations. Oddly enough, the mouth of the parrotfish is fused to its body, like the beak of a parrot.

Watch the coral reef change right before your eyes-observe the parrotfish as it constantly nibbles and reshapes the coral architecture. Searching for algae they are commonly seen grazing the corals for food. The parrotfish then manufactures sand by excreting the undigested rocks and coral particles. These fish play a crucial role in the coral reef ecosystem by converting the reef into sand.

Another interesting characteristic of some parrotfish is their ability to secrete a mucus cocoon surrounding themselves at night before going to "sleep". Although no one knows the exact reason why they do this, one theory is that the fish is trying to disguise its smell from nocturnal predators.

Stoplight Parrotfish
(terminal phase)

DIVER'S PEARL

Listen closely and you can hear the crunching sounds of the parrotfish nibbling on the coral reef.

Great Barracuda

BARRACUDA

Scuba Talk HAND SIGNAL

BARRACUDA

At the start of your dive, one of the first animals you may encounter is the **barracuda**. With its razor-sharp teeth and torpedo-shaped body, the barracuda is often seen hanging underneath a boat, awaiting a free meal. Barracudas may be seen so often by professional divers that they are given a pet name, such as "Fluffy"!

Barracudas swim in schools when they are small. Upon reaching adult size they usually become solitary animals. The great barracuda (*Sphyreana barracuda*) has been known to reach a size of up to six feet, with teeth reaching a length near one inch. Their curiosity often brings them close to divers and their menacing appearance can be intimidating. However, attacks are uncommon!

DIVER'S PEARL

The barracuda hunts usually at dusk and dawn when its gray body melds with the color of the gray water.

Foureye Butterflyfish

BUTTERFLYFISH

Butterflyfish are easily recognized by their small disk-like shape and vibrant color patterns. Some species of the butterflyfish have adapted an amazing strategy to deter attacks. For instance, the foureye (*Chaetodon capistratus*) and spotfin butterflyfish (*Chaetodon ocellatus*) have developed a "false eye" on the rear corners of the fish, so as to allure predators away from its true head.

Swimming with grace and beauty, these fish are frequently seen foraging on small coral polyps and any other bits and pieces of food they can find. Although fairly common, they photograph well and are often seen on book and magazine covers.

DIVER'S PEARL

Commonly seen swimming in pairs, many butterflyfish mate for life.

What's In A Name?

The following example illustrates how scientists classify all living animals into progressively more specific groupings based on structural traits. This is called the science of Taxonomy.

Common name: **Foureye butterflyfish**   Scientific name: *Chaetodon capistratus*

Kingdom	*Animalia*	All multicellular organisms which ingest food
Phylum	*Chordata*	Animals with backbones
Class	*Osteichthyes*	Bony fishes
Order	*Perciformes*	Largest fish order (example include butterflyfish, angelfish, mackerel, and blennies).
Family	*Chaedontidae*	Includes animals which have more similar structures than in Order. (examples include angelfish and butterflyfish
Genus	*Chaetodon*	Very similar characteristics but usually different members of the same genus are unable to reproduce or 'cross breed'. The genus includes all butterflyfish but the foureye cannot breed with the spotfin or banded.
Species	*capistratus*	The most specific, denotes animals which are able to reproduce and have offspring that appear similar to the adults. **Only** the foureye butterflyfish belongs in the species—*capistratus*

LOBSTER

The **Caribbean spiny lobster** (*Panulirus argus*) is probably best known for being a delicious meal. This lobster has no claws and is harmless. (Remember, it is illegal to catch the spiny lobster without proper permits). If given a chance to reach full maturity, this spiny lobster can grow to a size of up to two feet.

Lobsters are usually seen at night, crawling around the sandy bottom in search of food. During the day the lobsters hide in coral crevices and can be spotted by their protruding antennas. Lobsters can move quickly through the water by using their tails, which propel them backward into a crevice or away from predators.

Lobsters have an external skeleton which serves as armor against many predators. However, in order to grow larger, lobsters must molt their "armor" periodically.

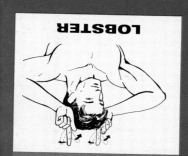

Scuba Talk HAND SIGNAL

LOBSTER

LOBSTER

DIVER'S PEARL

If attacked, the lobster will forgo a limb or claw to avoid being completely devoured, in the same way that lizards can shed their tails. Eventually the lost limb grows back, as does the lizard's tail.

Caribbean Spiny Lobster

Coral Crab

CRAB

CRAB

Scuba Talk HAND SIGNAL

CRAB

Crabs appear in more styles and varieties than you can imagine. Just look at the bright red color of the red reef crab (*Paguristes cadenati*)—a perfect example. The hermit crab is a small, interesting animal, which uses shells for protection. The hermit crab, much like a tenant, temporarily "rents" a particular shell until it grows too large, at which time it simply searches for a new, larger, vacant shell. Therefore, it could be said that no two hermit crab homes are alike.

DIVER'S PEARL

Closely related to insects and spiders, crabs are members of the largest phylum in the animal kingdom, Arthropoda, which contains approximately 200 million species.

Red Reef Hermit Crab

Porcelain and True crabs can be seen foraging (usually at night) over the coral bottom in search of food. These animals are scavengers, as are hermit crabs, and will eat just about anything they can get their claws on. Protected in a hard external skeleton, crabs have a formidable armor against many predators. However, in order to grow larger, crabs must periodically molt their shells. Needless to say, while molting, crabs are very vulnerable to attack.

TRUNKFISH

Scuba Talk HAND SIGNAL

TRUNKFISH

Smooth Trunkfish

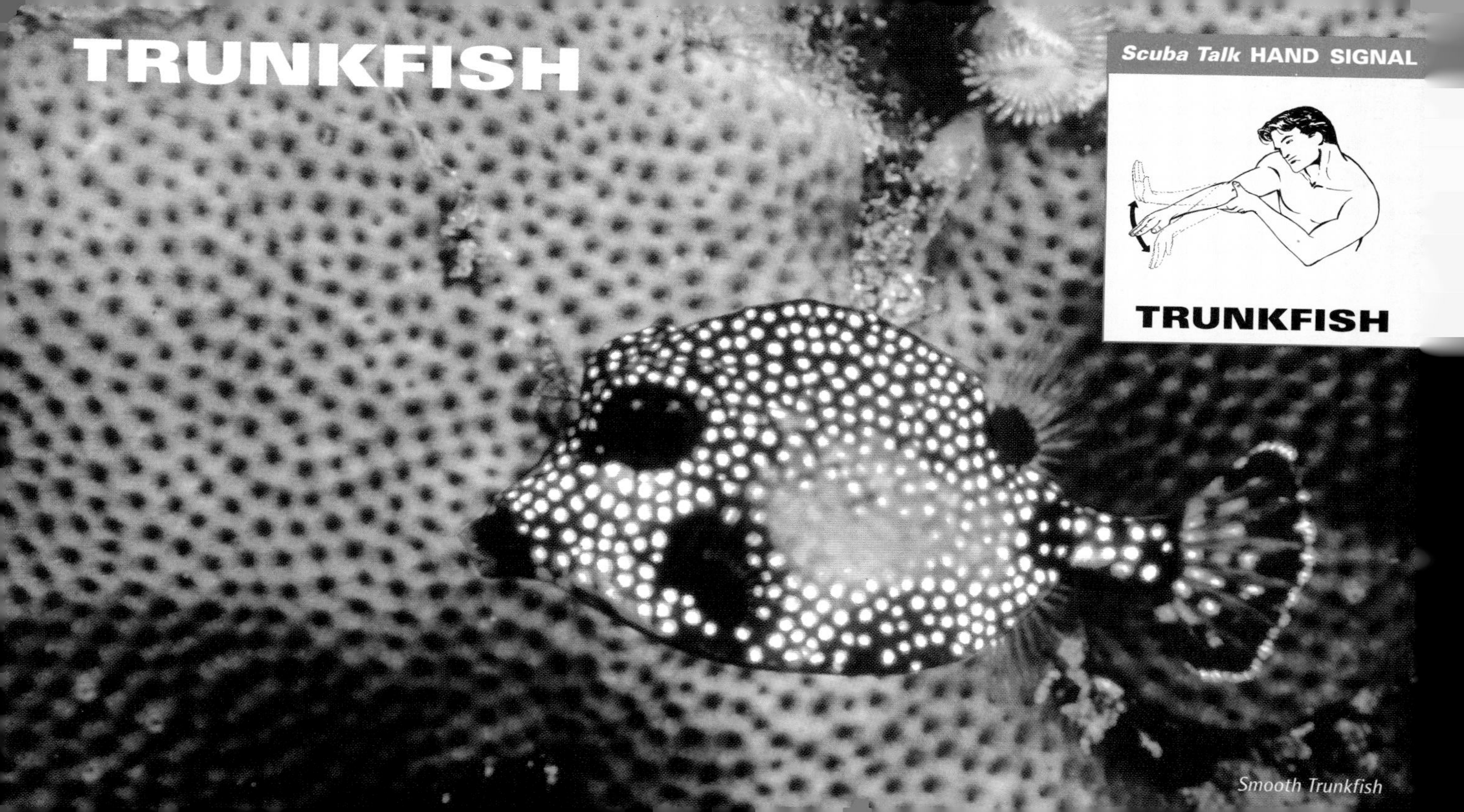

Boxfish, also known as **trunkfish**, are close relatives of the pufferfish. The trunkfish's bones form a box-like armor surrounding its body. In addition to their tough armor, these fish are protected by their ability to secrete a deadly toxic substance if threatened or highly stressed.

The smooth trunkfish (*Lactophrys triqueter*) shown above can frequently be seen while scuba diving in the Caribbean. Trunkfish feed on a variety of corals. In fact, some trunkfish blow water at the sandy bottom to uncover various worms, mollusks, and small crustaceans.

DIVER'S PEARL

Trunkfish are great fun to watch with their beautiful colors and their awkward swimming style. These fish certainly are not winning any races, but what's their hurry, they're in the Caribbean!

Reef Awareness

Whether dead or alive, all shells, coral, sand, and fish are an important part of a healthy reef ecosystem. Refrain from collecting or purchasing any products associated with the destruction of the coral reef. Adopt the attitude—look, but do not take or touch.

"CLEANING STATION"

"Cleaning stations" are one of the most sought-after symbiotic relationships for many fish of the coral reef community. Many fish infested with parasites come to these "cleaning stations" where parasitic fish including cleaner gobies, juvenile spanish hogfish (*Bodianus rufus*), juvenile bluehead wrasse (*Thalassoma bifasciatum*), and cleaner shrimp eat the parasites off the body of the infected fish. In fact, fish have so much trust in these "doctors of the reef" that they are often seen with mouths wide open and gills exposed to allow maximum cleaning in their most delicate spots. Ingeniously, one fish has mimicked the colors and behavior of the juvenile bluehead wrasse, but in fact is a phony! Instead of cleaning parasites, the wrasse blenny (*Hemiemblemaria simulus*) takes a bite out of the unsuspecting fish's body (watch your wrasse!). Fortunately, most cleaning fish are the real thing and provide an excellent service to the fish of the coral reef.

Cleaning Goby on Nassau Grouper

DIVER'S PEARLS

1. Great photo opportunities! Many fish go into a trance while being cleaned, allowing themselves to be approached at a close distance.

2. Anyone ask for a manicure? Just find the spotted cleaner shrimp (*Periclimenes yucatanicus*), and slowly place your hand near its reach. Remain motionless and the cleaner shrimp will begin cleaning your cuticles and nails free of charge.

Scuba Talk **HAND SIGNAL**

"CLEANING STATION"

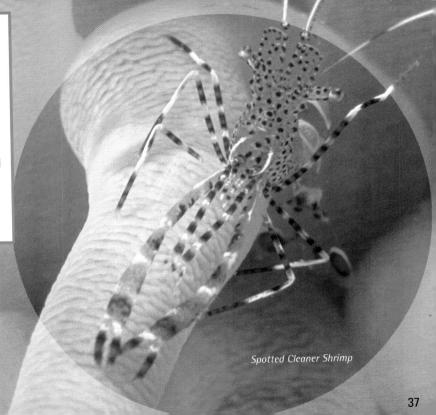

Spotted Cleaner Shrimp

Tiger Grouper

GROUPER

GROUPER

Scuba Talk **HAND SIGNAL**

How would you like to be a female during your younger years and then mature into a man? Well, this is exactly what happens to members of the **grouper** family.

Grouper are commonly seen hiding in recesses of the reef. These animals range in size, but certain species have the ability to grow large up to 700 pounds. They are carnivorous animals and have sharp, backward-pointing teeth. When a grouper strikes its prey, it opens its mouth wide. This creates suction, pulling the prey into the grouper's mouth.

DIVER'S PEARLS

1. Don't expect to see groupers in groups. The name—grouper—originated from the Portugese word *garupa*.

2. Ancient mariners believed that the large grouper could swallow a skin diver **whole**. Don't worry, you're *scuba* diving!

Nassau Grouper

Groupers are masters of color change. The grouper changes color based on mood and its surrounding environment. In fact, the Nassau grouper is said to have eight color phases.

Groupers are often seen in close proximity to divers. It is a common disbelief that Groupers like to be touched. This action frequently results in a diver being bitten. These animals are massive and can inflict wounds on divers, who often believe they understand the animal's behavior better than they really do.

SQUIRRELFISH

Squirrelfish are as nocturnal as night itself. Their eyes are large and black, an adaptation to aid night vision. At night these carnivorous fish are seen swimming around the reef in search of their prey. Squirrelfish are sensitive to underwater vibrations and smells, which enables the animal to navigate well at night.

Squirrelfish are commonly seen protecting their territory. They can be spotted during the daylight hours hiding in recesses of the reef. Their distinctive red color makes them easily identifiable day or night.

DIVER'S PEARL

The squirrelfish is named for its close resemblance to the red squirrel.

Reef Awareness

Today, unfortunately, oceans are used as a place for dumping large amounts of garbage, chemicals, etc. Do your part; please do not partake in throwing trash overboard.

Longspine Squirrelfish

Scuba Talk HAND SIGNAL

SQUIRRELFISH

41

These schooling fish
can be spotted even
before you jump
off the dive boat

SNAPPER

SNAPPER

Scuba Talk **HAND SIGNAL**

For years divers have thrown food into the water to attract fish. As a result, **Snappers** have become "socialized" to recognize the boat as an opportunity for a free meal. Snappers arrive at a dive boat soon after it anchors, and hang out until it leaves.

These fish have sharp teeth. However, they are usually harmless to man unless you are covered with food, in which case the snappers could inadvertently nip you in the process of pursuing a tasty morsel. The best way to avoid a problem is not to leave food on the boat (see "shark" and "barracuda" sections for reinforcement of this point!).

Swimming around corals, wrecks, and any area which offers some sort of protection, the beautiful yellowtail snapper (*Ocyurus chrysurus*), shown above is a common sight for divers.

DIVER'S PEARL

Due to their close swimming proximity, many divers make the mistake of reaching out to touch them. It's nearly impossible—look cool, don't even try—these fish are fast and seem to know exactly how close they can come to you in safety.

Spotted Drumfish

DRUMFISH

Scuba Talk HAND SIGNAL

DRUMFISH

Small and shy, **drumfish** are usually found in the cracks and crevices of the coral reef. The jackknife (*Equetus lanceolatus*) and spotteddrum (*Equetus punctatus*) are probably the two most common of the drumfish species. These animals are seen in three stages. The first is the juvenile, with the traditional long dorsal fin (this is to distract predators away from its real body). The next is the intermediate stage where the drumfish gains size and its dorsal fin begins to retract (probably due to predation). The third is the adult stage, when the animal reaches a size of up to one foot.

Consider yourself lucky if you come upon the drumfish; they are hard to find. Your best bet is on night dives.

DIVER'S PEARL

Drum fish are named for their ability to create drum-like sounds.

Reef Awareness

Corals are extremely delicate, the slightest touch by a diver's hand, fin, or body could easily damage the reef. Remember, corals grow slowly, what looks small may have taken years to have grown.

Spotted Filefish

FILEFISH

Scuba Talk HAND SIGNAL
FILEFISH

Filefish are thin boney fish which are closely related to triggerfish. One of the main differences between the two fish is that filefish, over time, lost the trigger mechanism so as to secure themselves in small hiding places. However, they have not lost the dorsal spine which is evident on the slender filefish (*Monacanthus tuckeri*) in the photograph to the right.

The whitespotted filefish (*Cantherhines macroceros*), shown above, can usually be seen swimming in pairs. Curious and cautious this filefish has been observed watching divers from behind its coral hiding places—so who is watching who?

DIVER'S PEARL

The skin of the filefish is as rough as sandpaper and once was used as an abrasive—which is how it got its name.

Slender Filefish

TRIGGERFISH

The **triggerfish** is named after its dorsal fin, which becomes erect when startled. When threatened, the fish darts into a small crevice and "triggers" its anal fin, thus anchoring itself into a hiding spot.

Their **diamond-shaped bodies,** **spectacular color patterns,** **unique swimming style** (it **swims with its dorsal and pectoral fins),** small but strong mouth, and large head make the triggerfish easily identifiable, and an enjoyable sighting for divers.

DIVER'S PEARL

"It's all fun and games until you lose an eye." The eyes of the triggerfish are strategically set towards the back of its head to avoid accidents when eating foods like sea urchins.

While diving, if you see plastic, aluminum cans, or any garbage floating in the ocean try and remove it. The fish will thank you.

Scuba Talk HAND SIGNAL

TRIGGERFISH

Ocean Triggerfish

GOATFISH

The **goatfish** has cleverly adapted two highly sensitive probes called *barbels* (not to be confused with barbells). These barbels hang directly underneath its chin and are used to find food such as mollusks, worms, and crustaceans that are buried in the sand.

These fish are commonly seen in small schools, swimming on the sandy bottoms of the coral reef. It is not unusual to see other small fish swimming behind the goatfish as it probes through the sand, hoping to obtain an easy meal.

DIVER'S PEARL

In ancient Rome, the goatfish was so prized as food that it had a value in silver equal to the price of a slave. It was served in a glass bowl—alive.

Grammar Test

You're in a school of spotted goatfish. Did you see many **fish** or many **fishes**?

Answer: You saw many fish.

Fish is the plural form when referring to more than one fish of the **same species**.

Fishes is the plural form when referring to more than one fish of **different species**.

PART TWO

"TRADITIONAL" HAND SIGNALS

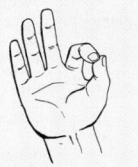

OK
Everything is OK.

UP

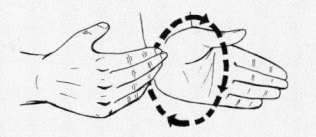

OUT OF AIR

AIR PRESSURE?

Amount of Air Pressure?—Your dive buddy is curious how much air is in your tank. Respond to this signal with one hand to show the amount of PSI in your tank. For example, each finger represents 100 PSI. Therefore the most you can show on one hand is 500 PSI. Thus, if you have 1,700 PSI, you would open and close your hand three times giving a total of 15 and then show two fingers, for a total of 1700 PSI (the amount that is in your tank).

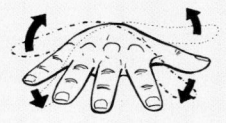

NOT OK
Something is Wrong—If something is wrong you must tell your dive buddy what is wrong. For example, your ear hurts, you're cold...etc.

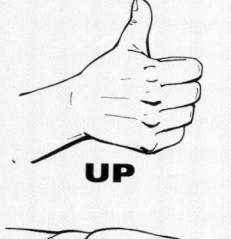

DOWN

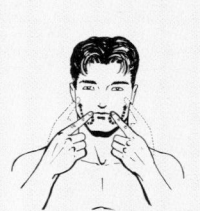

SMILE
Smile for a picture.

STOP

TIME?
Asking for the time. It may be used with other signals for example, time to ascend, or time to go back to the boat etc..

COOL
Everything is all right!

LOOK
Your dive buddy is trying to tell you to look at something.

BANG!
Making noise is an excellent way to gain the attention of your buddy.

BOAT
A diver is signaling – "where is the boat?" You may have to point this diver in the right direction.

TOO COOL!
To be used in conjunction with cool, meaning "too cool" this signal is appropriate when you see something extraordinary like a Manta ray!

PART THREE

PRE-TRIP CHECKLIST

☐ **Scuba Diving Certification Card!**

☐ Passport and visa

☐ Airplane ticket

Airline Carrier: _____

Time of Arrival: _____

Time of Departure: _____

☐ Hotel confirmation number

_____

☐ Car rental confirmation number

_____

☐ Credit cards

☐ Travelers Checks _____

check numbers:

$20: _____

$50: _____

$100: _____

☐ Trip itinerary _____

_____

_____

_____

☐ Important Names and Numbers:

_____

_____

_____

_____

PRE-DIVE EQUIPMENT CHECKLIST

DIVER'S PEARL

Be Prepared—we all know things get lost. Fill in this information so in the unlikely event that you lose your certification card, your file can easily be accessed.

Equipment

- [ ] Mask
- [ ] Fins
- [ ] Snorkel
- [ ] Wetsuit
- [ ] Booties
- [ ] Regulator
- [ ] Buoyancy compensator *(B.C.)*
- [ ] Dive computer or dive tables
- [ ] Timing device, e.g., dive watch or computer
- [ ] Weight belt and weights *(if not provided)*
- [ ] Tanks *(if not provided)*

Accessories

- [ ] Camera or video equipment *(don't forget plenty of film)*
- [ ] Dive light
- [ ] Compass
- [ ] Dive bag
- [ ] Dive knife
- [ ] Gloves *(optional)*
- [ ] Hood *(optional)*

Miscellaneous

- [ ] Sun tan lotion
- [ ] Towel
- [ ] Dry clothes
- [ ] Juice or water
- [ ] Snack

Certification Card Information

Name:_____

Certification Agency:_____

Level:_____

Student Identification #:_____

Instructor Name:_____

Instructor Certification #:_____

Date of Certification:_____

PERSONAL INFORMATION

NAME: _____

ADDRESS: _____

_____

PHONE #: _____ FAX #: _____

AGE: _____ HEIGHT: _____ WEIGHT: _____ BLOOD TYPE: _____

MEDICAL PROBLEMS: _____

_____

IN CASE OF EMERGENCY CONTACT: _____

ADDRESS: _____

PHONE #: _____ FAX #: _____

RELATIONSHIP: _____

PERSONAL PHYSICIAN: _____ PHONE #: _____

VACATION ADDRESS:

HOTEL NAME: _____

ADDRESS: _____

PHONE #: _____ ROOM #: _____

SCUBA BUDDIES

NAME: _____ *DIVE #: _____

ADDRESS: _____ DATE: _____

DIVE SITE: _____

PHONE #: _____ FAX #: _____

DIVE OPERATION: _____

BUDDY COMMENTS: _____

_____

NAME: _____ *DIVE #: _____

ADDRESS: _____ DATE: _____

DIVE SITE: _____

PHONE #: _____ FAX #: _____

DIVE OPERATION: _____

BUDDY COMMENTS: _____

_____

* Dive # can correspond to log sheet for reference

SCUBA BUDDIES

NAME: _____ *DIVE #: _____

ADDRESS: _____ DATE: _____

DIVE SITE: _____

PHONE #: _____ FAX #: _____

DIVE OPERATION: _____

BUDDY COMMENTS: _____

_____

NAME: _____ *DIVE #: _____

ADDRESS: _____ DATE: _____

DIVE SITE: _____

PHONE #: _____ FAX #: _____

DIVE OPERATION: _____

BUDDY COMMENTS: _____

_____

SCUBA BUDDIES

NAME: _____ *DIVE #: _____

ADDRESS: _____ DATE: _____

DIVE SITE: _____

PHONE #: _____ FAX #: _____

DIVE OPERATION: _____

BUDDY COMMENTS: _____

_____

NAME: _____ *DIVE #: _____

ADDRESS: _____ DATE: _____

DIVE SITE: _____

PHONE #: _____ FAX #: _____

DIVE OPERATION: _____

BUDDY COMMENTS: _____

_____

* Dive # can correspond to log sheet for reference

SCUBA BUDDIES

NAME: _____ *DIVE #: _____

ADDRESS: _____ DATE: _____

DIVE SITE: _____

PHONE #:_____ FAX #:_____

DIVE OPERATION: _____

BUDDY COMMENTS: _____

_____

NAME: _____ *DIVE #: _____

ADDRESS: _____ DATE: _____

DIVE SITE: _____

PHONE #:_____ FAX #:_____

DIVE OPERATION: _____

BUDDY COMMENTS: _____

_____

DIVE #	DATE	DIVE LOCATION	MAX DEPTH	VIS.	BOTTOM TIME	SHARK	RAY	EEL	BLOWFISH	ANGELFISH	TRUMPETFISH	SEA TURTLE	OCTOPUS	PARROTFISH	BARRACUDA	BUTTERFLYFISH	LOBSTER	CRAB	TRUNKFISH	"CLEANING STATION"	GROUPER	SQUIRRELFISH	SNAPPER	DRUMFISH	FILEFISH	TRIGGERFISH	GOATFISH	TOO COOL!	WITNESS

DIVE #	DATE	DIVE LOCATION	MAX DEPTH	VIS.	BOTTOM TIME	SHARK	RAY	EEL	BLOWFISH	ANGELFISH	TRUMPETFISH	SEA TURTLE	OCTOPUS	PARROTFISH	BARRACUDA	BUTTERFLYFISH	LOBSTER	CRAB	TRUNKFISH	"CLEANING STATION"	GROUPER	SQUIRRELFISH	SNAPPER	DRUMFISH	FILEFISH	TRIGGERFISH	GOATFISH	TOO COOL!	WITNESS

DIVE #	DATE	DIVE LOCATION	MAX DEPTH	VIS.	BOTTOM TIME	SHARK	RAY	EEL	BLOWFISH	ANGELFISH	TRUMPETFISH	SEA TURTLE	OCTOPUS	PARROTFISH	BARRACUDA	BUTTERFLYFISH	LOBSTER	CRAB	TRUNKFISH	"CLEANING STATION"	GROUPER	SQUIRRELFISH	SNAPPER	DRUMFISH	FILEFISH	TRIGGERFISH	GOATFISH	TOO COOL!	WITNESS

DIVE #							
DATE							
DIVE LOCATION							
MAX DEPTH							
VIS.							
BOTTOM TIME							
SHARK							
RAY							
EEL							
BLOWFISH							
ANGELFISH							
TRUMPETFISH							
SEA TURTLE							
OCTOPUS							
PARROTFISH							
BARRACUDA							
BUTTERFLYFISH							
LOBSTER							
CRAB							
TRUNKFISH							
"CLEANING STATION"							
GROUPER							
SQUIRRELFISH							
SNAPPER							
DRUMFISH							
FILEFISH							
TRIGGERFISH							
GOATFISH							
TOO COOL!							
WITNESS							

DIVE #	DATE	DIVE LOCATION	MAX DEPTH	VIS.	BOTTOM TIME	SHARK	RAY	EEL	BLOWFISH	ANGELFISH	TRUMPETFISH	SEA TURTLE	OCTOPUS	PARROTFISH	BARRACUDA	BUTTERFLYFISH	LOBSTER	CRAB	TRUNKFISH	"CLEANING STATION"	GROUPER	SQUIRRELFISH	SNAPPER	DRUMFISH	FILEFISH	TRIGGERFISH	GOATFISH	TOO COOL!	WITNESS

"QUIZ" FISH

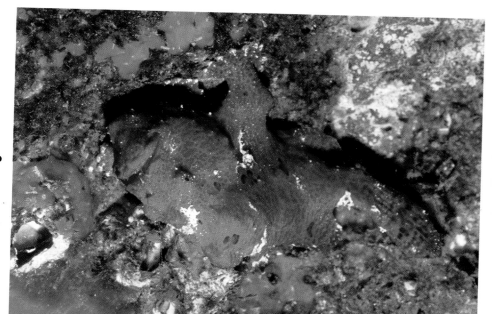

Correctly Identify this
"Quiz" fish
and
receive a coupon for
FREE
"Shipping & handling"
on your next purchase
of Scuba Talk.
Good Luck!

☐ **YES!** Please send me *Scuba Talk*™ @ **$14.95/book**

Charge my: ☐ VISA ☐ MasterCard

_____ ____/____
Credit Card #   Expiration Date

_____ _____
Print Name on Card   Signature

☐ Check for **total** amount $_____, is enclosed payable to Blue
Reef Publications, Inc.

Ship to:

_____
NAME

_____
ADDRESS

_____
CITY   STATE/PROVINCE

_____
COUNTRY   PHONE

($14.95) X (# books _____) =$ _____

Massachusetts Residents add 5% Sales Tax +$ _____

"Shipping and Handling"* +$ _____

TOTAL =$ _____

IDENTIFY "QUIZ" FISH _____
Look at the above picture for "quiz" fish details

* *"Shipping and Handling" (up to 5 books)*
Over 5 books or international address call or fax for shipping rates

US Book Rate $3.00; Priority Mail $4.50
Prices Continental US rates Only